# CONVERSATIONS WITH MOTHER

## BY MATTHEW LOMBARDO

# DPS

DRAMATISTS PLAY SERVICE

No one shall make any changes in this title(s) for the purpose of production. No part of this book may be reproduced, stored in a retrieval system, scanned, uploaded, or transmitted in any form, by any means, now known or yet to be invented, including mechanical, electronic, digital, photocopying, recording, videotaping, or otherwise, without the prior written permission of the publisher. No one shall share this title(s), or any part of this title(s), through any social media or file hosting websites.

For all inquiries regarding motion picture, television, online/digital and other media rights, please contact Concord Theatricals Corp.

## MUSIC AND THIRD-PARTY MATERIALS USE NOTE

Licensees are solely responsible for obtaining formal written permission from copyright owners to use copyrighted music and/or other copyrighted third-party materials (e.g. artworks, logos) in the performance of this play and are strongly cautioned to do so. If no such permission is obtained by the licensee, then the licensee must use only original music and materials that the licensee owns and controls. Licensees are solely responsible and liable for clearances of all third-party copyrighted materials, including without limitation music, and shall indemnify the copyright owners of the play(s) and their licensing agent, Concord Theatricals Corp., against any costs, expenses, losses and liabilities arising from the use of such copyrighted third-party materials by licensees. For music, please contact the appropriate music licensing authority in your territory for the rights to any incidental music.

## IMPORTANT BILLING AND CREDIT REQUIREMENTS

If you have obtained performance rights to this title, please refer to your licensing agreement for important billing and credit requirements.

*CONVERSATIONS WITH MOTHER* was first produced off Broadway by Bryan McCaffrey, BPM Theatrical, David Shapiro, Laura Z. Barket, Theatre Nerd Productions, Willette and Manny Klausner, Jim Jensen, Annaleise Loxton, and ShowTown Productions at Theatre 555 in New York City, opening on February 23, 2025. The performance was directed by Noah Himmelstein, with scenic design by Wilson Chin, lighting design by Elizabeth Harper, costume design by Ryan Park, sound design by John Gromada, wig design by Tom Watson, and projection design by Caite Hevner. The production stage manager was Christine Catti. The cast was as follows:

**MARIA COLLAVECHIO**........................... Caroline Aaron
**BOBBY COLLAVECHIO**............................... Matt Doyle

# CHARACTERS

**MARIA COLLAVECHIO** – (plays ages 37–76) Mother. Codependently obsessed with and involved in the life of her youngest son. Opinionated. Strong-willed. Affectionate yet tough. A survivor and a fixer. Although she exhibits a hard facade, there is an underlying and surprising vulnerability.

**BOBBY COLLAVECHIO** – (plays ages 8–65) Son. Handsome, masculine yet boyish. Dependent on his mother's approval and support. Constantly getting into trouble. A free spirit. Irresponsible and rudderless. Behind his attractive front lies a dark and unsettling insecurity.

# SETTING

Various locations, including New York City. Five decades.

# TIME FRAME

| Scene | Year | Maria's Age | Bobby's Age |
| --- | --- | --- | --- |
| Prologue | 1966 | 37 | 8 |
| Scene One | 1970 | 41 | 12 |
| Scene Two | 1974 | 45 | 16 |
| Scene Three | 1979 | 50 | 21 |
| Scene Four | 1984 | 55 | 26 |
| Scene Five | 1986 | 57 | 28 |
| Scene Six | 1992 | 63 | 34 |
| Scene Seven | 1992 | 63 | 34 |
| Scene Eight | 1993 | 64 | 35 |
| Scene Nine | 1998 | 69 | 40 |
| Scene Ten | 2004 | 75 | 46 |
| Scene Eleven | 2006 | 77 | 48 |
| Epilogue | TODAY | – | 65 |

# PRODUCTION NOTES

*Conversations with Mother* is performed without an intermission.

# Prologue

*(Lights up on* **MARIA COLLAVECHIO** *and* **BOBBY COLLAVECHIO**, *standing on opposite sides of the stage.)*

**BOBBY**.  Dear Mom: I hate camp. Can I come home? Love, Bobby.

**MARIA**.  Dear Bobby: N! O! Love, Your Mother.

**BOBBY**.  Dear Mom: I'm sad. Can I come home? Love, Bobby.

**MARIA**.  Dear Bobby: I'm sorry you're sad. But my answer is still no. Love, Your Mother.

**BOBBY**.  Dear Mom: One of the camp counselors asked me to stay with him in his van overnight. He has Strawberry Charleston Chews, clicker clackers and eyeglasses that have real X-ray vision. Can I stay with him some night? Love, Bobby.

**MARIA**.  Dear Bobby: Get packed! You're coming home!

# Scene One

## "Tell Me the Truth and I Won't Get Mad"

*(A telephone rings in the darkness.)*

**MARIA.** *(Calling.)* Frankie, turn that down before I break that record over your head!

*(Lights up on a frantic **MARIA**.)*

Hello?? (...) Yes, Operator. I'll accept the charges. Bobby?!

*(Lights up on **BOBBY**.)*

**BOBBY.** Mom?

**MARIA.** What happened? Where are you??

**BOBBY.** I ran away.

**MARIA.** You *what*?!

**BOBBY.** I did something bad so I ran away.

**MARIA.** Bobby, where are you?!

**BOBBY.** I can't tell. You'll get mad.

**MARIA.** I won't get mad.

**BOBBY.** You always get mad.

**MARIA.** I *won't* get mad!

**BOBBY.** Promise?

**MARIA.** Swear to God.

**BOBBY.** I'm in New York.

**MARIA.** *(Screaming.)* NEW YORK?!! Ohhh, you are in big trouble, mister. Big trouble!

*(He starts to cry in a high-pitched whine.)*

No-no. Okay. You're not in trouble. I'm sorry. You're not in trouble, sweetheart.

**BOBBY.** It wasn't my fault. It was Jimmy's idea.

**MARIA.** WHAT was Jimmy's idea?

**BOBBY.** Well. You know how you dropped us off this morning at Church because we were supposed to be altar boys at Miss Riberdy's wedding?

**MARIA.** Did you skip that Mass? Don't you tell me you skipped that Mass. If you skipped that Mass, I swear I'm going to pulverize you!

*(He whines again.)*

No-no. I'm sorry. Mommy's sorry.

**BOBBY.** You're mad.

**MARIA.** Nooo. Mommy's not mad. I just need you to tell me the truth. Can you do that?

**BOBBY.** I keep trying to but you keep getting mad.

**MARIA.** Then why don't we make a deal? You tell me the truth. And I won't get mad. Alright?

**BOBBY.** Alright.

**MARIA.** Okay?

**BOBBY.** Okay.

**MARIA.** Now what happened?

**BOBBY.** It was Jimmy's fault.

**MARIA.** It's always someone else's fault with you. Get on with it.

**BOBBY.** Well. Remember we didn't get to eat breakfast this morning? 'Cause Tippy pooped on the carpet? And you said you couldn't scrub shit and make pancakes at the same time 'cause we would all get staph infections? Remember you said that?

**MARIA**.  Vaguely.

**BOBBY**.  Well. Me and Jimmy were hungry. And we were in the dressing room at Church putting on our costumes –

**MARIA**.  *(Getting louder.)* You were in the *sacristy*, Bobby! It's not a dressing room. You weren't putting on costumes. You were in the sacristy putting on vestments! *Sacristy and vestments!*

(*He whines again.*)

I'm sorry. Sweetheart. I'm sorry.

**BOBBY**.  You're yelling.

**MARIA**.  No. Mommy's not yelling. She's just concerned. And worried. Concerned and worried. So. You and Jimmy were in the sacristy and you were hungry.

**BOBBY**.  And Jimmy said he knew where Father Frascadore kept all those bags of hosts.

**MARIA**.  Oh dear God no.

**BOBBY**.  So. We found the bag. And started eating them. They kind of taste like Nilla Wafers. But without the Nilla flavor. And not as crunchy. Mom?

**MARIA**.  Hmmmm?

**BOBBY**.  You still there?

**MARIA**.  Mmm-hmm.

**BOBBY**.  You mad?

**MARIA**.  *(Meaning no.)* Mmmm-mmmm.

**BOBBY**.  Good. 'Cause there's more.

**MARIA**.  *(Screaming.)* MOR– *(Then in a softer tone.)* Go on, sweetheart. Tell Mommy everything.

**BOBBY**.  Well. We ate half the bag. But then our throats got dry and kind of scratchy. So, then Jimmy remembered where Father Frascadore keeps the wine –

**MARIA**. Oh, for the love of Christ.

**BOBBY**. *(Continuing.)* – so we went upstairs and opened a bottle and began drinking it. Mom?

**MARIA**. Hmmmm?

**BOBBY**. You mad?

**MARIA**. *(Meaning no.)* Mmmm-mmmm.

**BOBBY**. Good. 'Cause there's more.

**MARIA**. *(Looks up to God.)* Slow day?

**BOBBY**. So we were getting really dizzy and feeling kind of silly. So that's when Jimmy – who always talks about being a doctor when he grows up – thought it might help him get into college – if he gave me like – a check-up. So. I took off my clothes. And Jimmy took off his. And that's when Father Frascadore walked in and told us –

(*He starts crying.*)

**MARIA**. That's when he told you what?

**BOBBY**. Father Frascadore told us –

(*He continues crying.*)

**MARIA**. Bobby, what did Father Frascadore say? It's alright. You can tell Mommy.

**BOBBY**. He told us we had to leave the Church and never come back because Jesus hates us now.

**MARIA**. *(With compassion.)* Oh, sweetheart.

**BOBBY**. Mommy, does Jesus hate me?

**MARIA**. No, Bobby. No. Of course not.

**BOBBY**. But Father Frascadore said –

**MARIA**. Father Frascadore is *wrong*.

**BOBBY**.  But he's a priest.

**MARIA**.  He's a *bad* priest. And a stupid man. Jesus doesn't hate anyone. He may be weeping a little right now.

**BOBBY**.  *(Hopeful.)* So. You're not mad?

**MARIA**.  *(Affectionately.)* No, my sweetheart. I am *not* mad.

**BOBBY**.  Good. 'Cause there's more.

**MARIA**.  *(Losing it.)* HOW CAN THERE BE MORE?!! YOU HAVE JUST DONE ALL THE THINGS I HAVE TAUGHT YOU NOT TO DO IN LESS THAN FIVE HOURS! THAT'S ONE VENIAL SIN EVERY FIFTEEN MINUTES!

**BOBBY**.  You promised you wouldn't get mad!

**MARIA**.  I LIED! That's what mothers do! We LIE to our children hoping and praying that we can somehow scare the shit out of them in the slightest hope they stay on the right path! But my son?? NOOOO!! He has to go get drunk and play with his best friend's pee-pee while eating unblessed hosts IN A FUCKING SACRISTY!!

**BOBBY**.  Am I like in trouble?

**MARIA**.  No Bobby. You are not *like* in trouble. You, my beloved son and thankfully last born *are* in trouble! Like no other boy has ever been in trouble before! Your punishment will go down in the history books as the best sentencing a mother has ever given a child WITHOUT BEING CONVICTED OF A FELONY!! Now what else??

**BOBBY**.  Huh?

**MARIA**.  What else? What else? How did you get to New York?

**BOBBY**.  Oh. Well. Jimmy thought –

**MARIA.** Listen to me, mister. I am on the verge of obtaining a severe mental illness right now. I have five other kids at home and a dog who is incontinent. If you mention Jimmy's name one more time, and I do mean ONE. MORE. TIME – *(In a darkened tone.) there may not be a dog alive when you get home.* See where I'm going with this?

**BOBBY.** *(Creeped out.)* I think so.

**MARIA.** Good. Now. How did you get from Connecticut to New York?

**BOBBY.** We took the bus.

**MARIA.** Where did you get the money to take the bus?

**BOBBY.** Well, Jimmy thought –

**MARIA.** Bobby, I mean it! I've got Tippy on a choke collar. I can finish him off by the time I stop speaking this sentence! *(Pointedly.)* Where. Did you get. The money. For the bus?

*(Beat and then:)*

**BOBBY.** *(Remorsefully.)* I sold the gold crucifix you and Daddy got me for my communion. I didn't think you'd let me come back home. So, I sold my cross to get tickets for me and – you know who. That's why I ran away. 'Cause I thought you and Daddy would hate me. Just like Jesus does.

*(Pause.)*

**MARIA.** *(Her heart breaking.)* Ohhh, my boy. My silly, sweet, *criminal* of a baby boy.

**BOBBY.** I didn't mean to hurt no one.

**MARIA.** I know you didn't.

**BOBBY.** I really am sorry.

**MARIA.** I know you are.

**BOBBY.** Do you still love me?

**MARIA.** Not at this moment.

**BOBBY.** Am I going to be punished?

**MARIA.** Beaten within an inch of your LIFE!

## Scene Two

## "I Know What You're Doing Before You Even Do It"

(*BOBBY* enters as *MARIA* is sitting reading a magazine.)

**BOBBY**.  Hey Ma.

**MARIA**.  Hi sweetheart. You have a good time with your friends at the beach today?

**BOBBY**.  Yeah. Thanks for letting me take the car. I filled up the tank. I'll wash it tomorrow when I get home from school.

**MARIA**.  You're such a good boy.

**BOBBY**.  Dad go to bed already?

**MARIA**.  (*Nods.*) He has an early day tomorrow.

**BOBBY**.  I think I'm gonna go up myself. I'm pretty beat. Night, Ma.

**MARIA**.  Goodnight, my sweetheart.

(*He kisses her and starts to exit.*)

Oh, Bobby?

(*He stops, turns back.*)

You *did* go to Church this morning.

**BOBBY**. Yeah.

**MARIA**.  'Cause that was our deal. You go to Church. And I give you the car for the rest of the day so that you could go to the beach with your friends.

**BOBBY**.  And that's what happened.

**MARIA.**  Because your older brother? He always thought he was smarter than me. You know what he would do? He would stop by the Church, pick up a bulletin and then use the money I gave him for the Offertory to go buy cigarettes.

**BOBBY.**  *(Uncomfortable.)* Oh. That is. So. Not. Cool.

**MARIA.**  No. It wasn't. And I don't know what hurt me more. The fact that he didn't go to Church. *(Pointedly.)* Or that he lied to his very own mother.

**BOBBY.**  Oh. Yeah. That's bad.

**MARIA.**  I'm so glad I don't have to worry about that with you.

**BOBBY.**  Me too.

(**BOBBY** *starts off, she stops him.)*

**MARIA.**  We live in such a quaint little town. Everyone knows everyone. Everyone sees everything. That's how your brother got caught. Mrs. Buttafuoco from next door? She was buying the Sunday paper at Revco and saw him walking out with a pack of Marlboros.

**BOBBY.**  And she told you?

**MARIA.**  Oh yeah.

**BOBBY.**  And you punished him?

**MARIA.**  Nope.

**BOBBY.**  Why not?

**MARIA.**  Because I figured – if he could look his own mother in the face and not tell her the truth? Well. That was *my* fault. I obviously didn't teach him any better. *(Directly.)* For him to not know the difference between right and wrong.

(**BOBBY** *senses she knows something.)*

You okay, sweetheart? You look a little flushed.

**BOBBY.** Probably just all the sun I got today.

**MARIA.** You better get some rest then.

(**BOBBY** *starts to rush off, she stops him.*)

Oh, Bobby? I know you're tired and want to get to bed. But did you happen to get a parking ticket today?

**BOBBY.** What?

**MARIA.** Oh, I'm sorry. Am I not speaking clearly?

**BOBBY.** No. I mean.

**MARIA.** Because when you asked "what" – either you didn't understand the question or I wasn't speaking clearly.

**BOBBY.** *(Getting flustered.)* I understood the question.

**MARIA.** Then why did you ask "what"? Maybe you needed a bit more time. You couldn't remember if you got a parking ticket. Although if I got a parking ticket when using my parents' car, that's something I probably would remember.

**BOBBY.** *(Trying to save himself.)* You know, come to think of it. I *did* get a parking ticket today.

**MARIA.** *(Playing along.)* Did you now?

**BOBBY.** It must have just slipped my mind.

**MARIA.** Of course.

**BOBBY.** But I'm going to pay for it, Ma. Don't worry.

**MARIA.** Do I look worried?

**BOBBY.** No.

**MARIA.** Okay then.

**BOBBY.** Okay then.

(*He starts off, then:*)

**MARIA.**  Oh, Bobby? Sorry to bother you again but one last question. Where did you *get* that parking ticket?

**BOBBY.**  What?

**MARIA.**  Where?

**BOBBY.**  Where?

**MARIA.**  Where.

**BOBBY.**  Like what street?

**MARIA.**  Like what street.

**BOBBY.**  I don't know. It was. Umm. A street by the beach?

(*Beat.*)

**MARIA.**  (*Clearly disappointed.*) Goodnight, Bobby.

(*He starts off. She does not stop him this time.*)

**BOBBY.**  I guess I'll go to bed now.

**MARIA.**  Mmm-hmm.

**BOBBY.**  You don't want to ask me anything else?

**MARIA.**  Uhh-uhh.

**BOBBY.**  Alright?

**MARIA.**  Alright.

**BOBBY.**  Okay?

**MARIA.**  Okay.

**BOBBY.**  Goodnight?

**MARIA.**  Goodnight.

(**BOBBY** *exits.*)

(*To herself.*) Three. Two. One.

(**BOBBY** *storms back into the room.*)

**BOBBY.** *(Increasingly crazy and defensive.)* I KNOW YOU KNOW EVERYTHING SO LET'S JUST GET IT ALL OUT IN THE OPEN! I DIDN'T GO TO CHURCH! I MEAN I *DID* GO TO CHURCH. BUT ONLY TO PICK UP THAT STUPID BULLETIN TO MAKE YOU THINK I WAS THERE! WANNA KNOW WHAT ELSE I DID? I WENT TO A LIQUOR STORE. BUT I PARKED TWO STREETS OVER SO NO ONE WOULD SEE DADDY'S CAR BEFORE I PAID SOMEONE TO BUY ME BEER. THAT'S RIGHT! I. BOUGHT. BEER! BUT WHEN I GOT BACK TO THE CAR, I GOT A TICKET 'CAUSE I FORGOT THERE WAS NO FRIGGIN' STREET PARKING ON SUNDAYS! OH, AND ANOTHER THING? I DIDN'T GO TO THE BEACH WITH MY FRIENDS. I WENT TO A POOL PARTY. ALONE. AND IT WASN'T JUST ANY POOL PARTY. THIS WAS A POOL PARTY – *WITHOUT GIRLS!* IN RHODE ISLAND! I TOOK THE CAR OUT OF STATE AND WHEN I GOT HOME, I TURNED BACK THE ODOMETER WITH A SCREWDRIVER SO YOU WOULDN'T FIND OUT HOW FAR I ACTUALLY DROVE! *SO THERE IT IS, LADY!* THERE IT ALLLLL IS. I SKIPPED CHURCH. GOT A PARKING TICKET. LIED ABOUT THE BEACH. DRANK. DROVE. SMOKED POT. SWAM NAKED. AND I KISSED THREE DIFFERENT BOYS WHOSE NAMES I DELIBERATELY NEVER BOTHERED TO FIND OUT!!

(*Beat.*)

So. What do you have to say to all that?

(*Beat and then:*)

**MARIA.** Now we can get some sleep!

## Scene Three

## "Did You Get a Job Yet?"

*(The telephone rings. Lights up on* **BOBBY.***)*

**BOBBY.** Hello?

*(Lights up on* **MARIA.***)*

**MARIA.** Oh, thank God! I've been calling every hospital in New York!

**BOBBY.** I just left six hours ago.

**MARIA.** You could be dead in six minutes.

**BOBBY.** That's encouraging.

**MARIA.** What have you been doing all this time?

**BOBBY.** Unpacking.

**MARIA.** What's to unpack? You're living in one room.

**BOBBY.** It's called a studio.

**MARIA.** Did you go to that interview?

**BOBBY.** Just came back. I got the job!

**MARIA.** *(Thrilled.)* Oh that's wonderful!

**BOBBY.** I start tonight.

**MARIA.** Not so wonderful.

**BOBBY.** What's wrong?

**MARIA.** You're working at night?

**BOBBY.** Yeah. So what?

**MARIA.** The only people that work at night are hookers and derelicts.

**BOBBY.** Well, if this job doesn't work out, it's nice to know I still have two other options.

**MARIA.** Where is this new job?

**BOBBY.** It's at a place called The Meat Hook.

**MARIA.** What is it? A delicatessen?

**BOBBY.** It's a bar.

**MARIA.** *(Disapproving.)* Oh Bobby.

**BOBBY.** You told me to take anything.

**MARIA.** Anything meaning a nice day job.

**BOBBY.** I need to write during the day.

**MARIA.** You can't write during the night?

**BOBBY.** Ma. I need money right now. And I don't exactly have that many skills.

**MARIA.** Whose fault is that? Your father and I told you to go to college. We *begged* you to go to college.

**BOBBY.** Please don't start.

**MARIA.** All your other friends went to college. Danny Spineti. Johnny Massaro. Oh, and Jimmy Bonomo? The boy you used to play doctor with? He actually became – *a doctor*!

**BOBBY.** Ma.

**MARIA.** You could have had a good life working construction with your brothers.

**BOBBY.** That life's not me.

**MARIA.** Course not. You'd rather work with hookers and derelicts at a place called The Meat Hook which doesn't even serve sandwiches.

**BOBBY.** Anything else?

*(Beat.)*

MARIA.  *(Heartfelt.)* I miss you.

BOBBY.  I've only been gone a few hours.

MARIA.  I can miss in that amount of time. When you started school? I would miss you before you even got on the bus. And I'd be waiting for you every day when you got off.

BOBBY.  I remember.

MARIA.  I was a good mother to you.

BOBBY.  Why are you talking in past tense?

MARIA.  Because I'm not always gonna be around.

BOBBY.  You've been saying that since I was five.

MARIA.  I just want you to be prepared.

BOBBY.  For what?

MARIA.  *Life.*

(*He speaks in a different tone, gentler.*)

BOBBY.  Why don't you go to a movie or do something tonight?

MARIA.  It's too soon. I need to finish these cards.

BOBBY.  Ask someone to come over and help.

MARIA.  I'm the widow. They have to be written by me.

BOBBY.  No one will know.

MARIA.  Everyone will know.

BOBBY.  Who?

MARIA.  People.

BOBBY.  What people?

MARIA.  People-people.

BOBBY.  Ma.

**MARIA.** Go finish unpacking.

**BOBBY.** Ma!

**MARIA.** What?!

*(Beat and then:)*

*(Surprisingly vulnerable.)* We had such plans. Travel. Cruises. Second homes. And then? The very day your father finally *does* decide to retire? He gets this cough that won't go away. Six months later? I'm holding the hand of a man I don't even recognize 'cause of all that poison those doctors shot into his system. Twelve months go by? We're dancing again, celebrating like fools – *remission.* Eighteen months later? I'm buying a black dress that doesn't fit and sitting beside a casket for days until it's finally lowered into the ground. Gone. It all just – *disappears.*

**BOBBY.** You want me to come back home?

**MARIA.** Don't you dare. You just get settled in that studio of yours and become that "play-writer" you want to be.

**BOBBY.** It's "playwright," Ma, not "play-writer."

**MARIA.** You want to write plays?

**BOBBY.** Yeah.

**MARIA.** Then you're a "play-writer."

**BOBBY.** Let me go. I gotta poop and take a shower.

**MARIA.** Shower? You don't start work for another few hours.

**BOBBY.** I always shower after I poop. Don't you?

**MARIA.** No.

**BOBBY.** How do you get clean?

**MARIA.** I use toilet paper like the rest of the free world.

**BOBBY**.  I don't like toilet paper.

**MARIA**.  What do you use if you don't use toilet paper?

**BOBBY**.  Coolie wipes.

**MARIA**.  Coolie whats?

**BOBBY**.  Coolie wipes.

**MARIA**.  You use coolie wipes then take a shower?

**BOBBY**.  Yeah.

**MARIA**.  Oh, Bobby, there is something very wrong with you.

**BOBBY**.  I like being clean.

**MARIA**.  You're not supposed to be that clean.

**BOBBY**.  I gotta go.

**MARIA**.  That's why you're sick all the time.

**BOBBY**.  Goodbye, Ma.

**MARIA**.  You have no bacteria.

**BOBBY**.  I'm hanging up now.

**MARIA**.  People die when they have no bacteria.

**BOBBY**.  Love you.

**MARIA**.  That's how Tippy died. He had no bacteria.

**BOBBY**.  Tippy died because you killed him.

**MARIA**.  I did not kill Tippy!

**BOBBY**.  You took him to the Humane Society and they put him down.

**MARIA**.  *I took Tippy to a farm!*

**BOBBY**.  I'm hanging up now.

**MARIA**.  You really should talk to someone.

**BOBBY.** Goodnight, Ma.

**MARIA.** A professional. Someone who knows about bacteria.

**BOBBY.** I'll call you tomorrow.

**MARIA.** Don't you lose that job!

## Scene Four

## "Why Can't You Ever Meet a Nice Boy?"

*(A telephone rings. Lights up on* **BOBBY***, bartending.)*

**BOBBY**.  Meat Hook.

*(Lights up on* **MARIA***, wearing a nightgown.)*

**MARIA**.  Hi sweetheart.

**BOBBY**.  Ma. What's wrong?

**MARIA**.  Why does something have to be wrong?

**BOBBY**.  It's two o'clock in the morning and you're calling me at work.

**MARIA**.  I couldn't sleep. So, I thought who else would be up at this godforsaken hour? And then I remembered: my son works at a delicatessen.

**BOBBY**.  It's not a delicatessen.

**MARIA**.  Well, I'm telling people it is. So, if anyone asks: *know your meats.*

**BOBBY**.  *(Laughs.)* What are you doing?

**MARIA**.  I'm watching the QVC.

**BOBBY**.  It's just QVC, Ma. There's no "the."

**MARIA**.  They have these nice, frozen Cornish hens on sale that I'm going to get everyone for Christmas.

**BOBBY**.  Please don't buy poultry on QVC.

**MARIA**.  They'll make cute stocking stuffers.

**BOBBY**.  They won't.

**MARIA.**  Which one do you want? They come in white, dark or buff.

**BOBBY.**  I don't want.

**MARIA.**  White, dark or buff?

**BOBBY.**  What?

**MARIA.**  White, dark or buff?

**BOBBY.**  I don't even know what you're talking about.

**MARIA.**  I'll get you the buff.

**BOBBY.**  *(Smiles.)* You got plans tomorrow?

**MARIA.**  Ughh. I got the grandkids coming over.

**BOBBY.**  Awww.

**MARIA.**  No awwww. They drive me freakin' crazy. Who's spilling grape juice on my nice white carpet. Who's muckin' mud on my clean tile floor. And if your nephews keep peeing on my toilet seat? Next time you see them? They're gonna be your nieces!

**BOBBY.**  They're kids, Ma.

**MARIA.**  They're pigs and animals. Every last one of them.

**BOBBY.**  Then don't have them over.

**MARIA.**  So. Who was that?

**BOBBY.**  Who was what?

**MARIA.**  I left a message with this fella who answered your phone this morning.

**BOBBY.**  I never got the message.

**MARIA.**  And I never got an answer to my question.

**BOBBY.**  Which was?

**MARIA.**  Who answered your phone this morning?

**BOBBY.**  Dirk.

**MARIA.**  Dirk? What's a Dirk??

**BOBBY.**  This guy I met last week.

**MARIA.**  *(Disapproving.)* Oh, Bobby. You met him last week and you're already sleeping with him?

**BOBBY.**  No. I slept with him last week when I met him.

**MARIA.**  You know when I first slept with your father? Our wedding night. And you wanna know how I found out about sex? The priest who married us. He gave me a pamphlet after the reception. It was called "How to Be A Good Christian Wife." It had instructions and diagrams. It fucking scared the shit out of me.

**BOBBY.**  Times have changed, Ma.

**MARIA.**  *Having a good moral compass never changes.* I'm not saying that I don't want you to find someone, Bobby. I do. I just don't want you to be so free with your business. Get to know this one first. Then if you like him and he likes you and you both think there's some kind of future? Then you can play with each other's *fanooks.* Is he at least Italian?

**BOBBY.**  German.

**MARIA.**  Doctor?

**BOBBY.**  Actor.

**MARIA.**  Working?

**BOBBY.**  Unemployed.

**MARIA.**  Why don't you just get a machete and chop me into little bits?

**BOBBY.**  Ma, it's really starting to get busy here and –

**MARIA.**  You know what the Germans are famous for? Baking people like crescent rolls.

**BOBBY.**  Would you stop? I like this guy. He's really talented.

**MARIA.** How do you know? What? Does he do monologues for you every night??

**BOBBY.** Arggghhhh.

**MARIA.** If this Dirk person has no job, how does he live?

**BOBBY.** I think his parents send him money.

**MARIA.** Oh. So the two of you have something in common.

**BOBBY.** You never like any of the guys I date.

**MARIA.** That's because you get involved with more disasters than State Farm Insurance!

**BOBBY.** That's not true.

**MARIA.** Oh no? What about that freak you dated who was into M&Ms?

**BOBBY.** It was S&M. And he was diabetic.

**MARIA.** I just don't understand what you have against nice guys. The guys who believe in God and love their mothers. But I don't think you like those guys because I don't think you like *you*!

**BOBBY.** Ma, I gotta go. My manager is giving me dirty looks and –

**MARIA.** *(Quickly, desperately.)* I MISS HIS SNORING!

*(Beat.)*

*(A vulnerable admission.)* That's why I can never sleep. I miss his snoring. Your father used to snore so loud and so long. When we first got married? I couldn't stand it. I would keep waking him up. Have him sleep on his side. On his stomach. Some nights I just wanted to take a pillow to his face and snuff the life out of him. But. Then. I don't know. I guess. I got used to it. It gave me a – a – comfort. Because I knew someone was there.

**BOBBY.**  *(Rejecting.)* Ma, I really do need to go.

**MARIA.**  *(Hurt.)* Oh. Yeah. *(Covering.)* Sure sweetheart. You go. I just. I just wanted to hear your voice. I just wanted to hear – some *noise*.

## Scene Five

## "If Everyone Jumped Off a Bridge, Would You?"

*(Lights up on* **BOBBY** *as a telephone rings.)*

**BOBBY**. Hey Ma.

*(Lights up on* **MARIA**.*)*

**MARIA**. Bobby, hold on. I got your sister on the other line.

*(Click.)*

Gina, I gotta go. Your brother's on the phone.

**BOBBY**. It's still me.

**MARIA**. Still who?

**BOBBY**. Bobby.

**MARIA**. What are you doing on this line?

**BOBBY**. You didn't click off.

**MARIA**. Hold on.

*(Click.)*

Gina?

**BOBBY**. It's still me.

*(Click.)*

**MARIA**. Gina?

**BOBBY**. Still me.

*(Click.)*

**MARIA**. Gina?

**BOBBY**. Me.

**MARIA.** Hold on. Let me just say goodbye to your sister.

(*Click.*)

Gina?

**BOBBY.** Would you stop with the Ginas already?!

**MARIA.** Why are you yelling at me?

**BOBBY.** I'm not yelling.

**MARIA.** Why are you calling then?

**BOBBY.** I'm returning your call.

**MARIA.** Did I call you?

**BOBBY.** Yeah.

**MARIA.** What did I want?

**BOBBY.** I don't know. That's why I'm calling you!

**MARIA.** Well, you're confusing me! And I can only talk for another three minutes. Felicia Gallant is going through a very difficult time right now and I need to be there for her.

**BOBBY.** Who the hell is Felicia Gallant?

**MARIA.** You remember Felicia. (*In one breath.*) She was married to Mitch and then their marriage hit the skids so Mitch cheated on her and then she cheated on him and then they finally got divorced but then she got back together with Lucas and married him but now Lucas has just been shot and he's been in the hospital for weeks and Felicia is just heartbroken.

**BOBBY.** Why do you watch that crap??

**MARIA.** My stories are not crap! *They are blueprints on how to live life in the face of adversity.*

**BOBBY.** Yeah. Well. Speaking of adversity, I got some bad news.

**MARIA.** *(Immediately freaking out.)* OH MY GOD! YOU HAVE THE AIDS!

**BOBBY.** NO!

**MARIA.** THAT GERMAN GAVE YOU THE AIDS!

**BOBBY.** I don't have AIDS!

**MARIA.** THAT'S WHAT GERMANS DO! THEY GIVE YOU THE AIDS!

**BOBBY.** No one's giving me AIDS!

**MARIA.** So you don't have the AIDS?

**BOBBY.** Would you stop putting the word "the" in front of AIDS?

**MARIA.** If you don't have the AIDS then what's your bad news?

**BOBBY.** I lost my job.

**MARIA.** *(Relieved.)* THANK YOU SACRED HEART OF JESUS!

**BOBBY.** They fired me.

**MARIA.** What did you do?

**BOBBY.** Nothing.

**MARIA.** Did you steal?

**BOBBY.** No.

**MARIA.** You stole.

**BOBBY.** Ma.

**MARIA.** You stole money.

**BOBBY.** I didn't steal money.

**MARIA.** You used to steal money out of my own pocketbook. Why wouldn't you steal money from a delicatessen?

**BOBBY.** I was nine then and *it's not a delicatessen*!

MARIA.  Well, it should be! A place called The Meat Hook should at least serve cold cuts!

BOBBY.  *(Desperate.)* DAMMIT, MA! I NEED MONEY!

(*Beat.*)

MARIA.  Oh.

BOBBY.  I feel bad asking you.

MARIA.  No, you don't.

BOBBY.  I'll pay you back.

MARIA.  No, you won't.

BOBBY.  So. Will you?

MARIA.  What about your boyfriend Dirk? He can't help you out? No wait. He can't. He's still unemployed.

BOBBY.  Feel better?

MARIA.  How much do you need?

BOBBY.  Three hundred dollars.

MARIA.  I'll send you five.

BOBBY.  You mad?

MARIA.  Not really.

BOBBY.  Good. 'Cause there's more.

MARIA.  There always *is*.

BOBBY.  It wasn't my fault.

MARIA.  It never *is*.

BOBBY.  Just hear me out.

MARIA.  No-no-no-no-no. This is going to be fun. Let me tell *you* what happened: Someone came up with a really great idea and you went along with it. But in the end, it turned out *not* to be such a great idea and *you* were the one who got in trouble for it.

**BOBBY.** It's as if you were *there*!

**MARIA.** So let's hear it. I'm already disappointing Felicia.

**BOBBY.** So. There's this guy. At work. Billy. And Billy thought that if we rang up drinks into the cash register for fifty cents less than what they actually were, we could make an extra fifty cents for each customer in tips –

**MARIA.** Bobby. I don't have time to get all fittutzed with you today. Cut to the chase and tell me how much you need so the owner doesn't press charges.

**BOBBY.** How did you know that's what the owner is going to do?

**MARIA.** Because I have been bailing you kids out for years. My girls? No problems at all. My boys? They knock down the Ten Commandments as if they were bowling pins. How much more do you need?

**BOBBY.** Another five hundred.

**MARIA.** What a coincidence. Is that just your share?

**BOBBY.** No. Billy doesn't have to pay.

**MARIA.** Oh, I can't wait to hear this one.

**BOBBY.** Billy told the owner that I was the one stealing money. And he also slept with him.

**MARIA.** Another pig and animal.

**BOBBY.** So. Will you help me? Please.

**MARIA.** I will Western Union you the five hundred in the morning.

**BOBBY.** You mean a thousand.

**MARIA.** I mean five hundred.

**BOBBY.** Ma, if you only send me five hundred, I won't have money to live.

**MARIA.**  Then you better find yourself another job.

**BOBBY.**  But.

**MARIA.**  Upp. There's my other line.

**BOBBY.**  Ma!

**MARIA.**  Goodbye.

*(Dial tone.)*

## Scene Six

## "What Do You Want For Your Birthday?"

*(The sound of people singing "Happy Birthday" can be heard. At the end of the song there is clapping and yelling. We hear the following:)*

**BOBBY.** *(Voice-over.)* Hey. You've reached Bobby Collavechio. You know what to do when you hear the beep.

*(Beep. Lights up on* **MARIA** *in a spotlight.)*

**MARIA.** Sweetheart, it's Ma. We're just about to sit down to supper. Where are you? Should we wait? Give me a call and let me know what time you're going to be here. Love you.

**BOBBY.** *(Voice-over.)* Hey. You've reached Bobby Collavechio. You know what to do when you hear the beep.

*(Beep. Another light finds* **MARIA.***)*

**MARIA.** Bobby, it's Ma. Why aren't you answering your phone? You should have been here hours ago. Did something happen? We just cut the cake so I'll save you a piece. Call me, sweetheart. I'm starting to get worried.

**BOBBY.** *(Voice-over.)* Hey. You've reached Bobby Collavechio. You know what to do when you hear the beep.

*(Beep. And another.)*

**MARIA.** It's Ma. Again. Everyone just left. All the kids kept asking where you were but I didn't know what to tell them because I don't know what you're doing. Bobby. Call me. Please.

*(Beep. Another.)*

**BOBBY**. *(Voice-over.)* Hey. You've reached Bobby Collavechio. You know what to do when you hear the beep.

**MARIA**.  Sweetheart, what's going on? It's not like you not to call me back. I would appreciate a call. Unless you're dead. Bobby, call me and let me know you're not dead. I don't understand any of this. Bobby. *Call me!*

## Scene Seven

## "You Can't Pull the Wool Over My Eyes"

*(Lights up on* **MARIA***, still wearing her overcoat, seated on a chair in Bobby's apartment. After a moment passes,* **BOBBY** *enters. He has a large, visible bruise on his cheek. His demeanor is questionable.)*

**BOBBY.** What are you doing here?

**MARIA.** I was in the neighborhood.

*(Beat.)*

**BOBBY.** How'd you get in?

**MARIA.** I'm a mother. There's not a lock I don't know how to pick.

*(Beat.)*

**BOBBY.** Tell me you didn't go through my things.

**MARIA.** *(Letting him know she did.)* I didn't go through your th–

*(She makes eye contact with him, sees the bruise.)*

What's going on there?

**BOBBY.** What?

**MARIA.** Don't play dumb with me. What happened to your face?

*(Beat.)*

**BOBBY.** *(Redirecting.)* Sorry I missed your birthday.

**MARIA.** You could have called.

**BOBBY**. Yeah. But.

**MARIA**. You could. Have called.

**BOBBY**. Yeah.

> *(An awkward silence.)*

> *(Redirects again.)* So how was your party?

**MARIA**.  The cake was dry. The gifts were unnecessary. And your nieces are now dressing like prostitutes.

> *(Beat.)*

How long you gonna keep this a secret?

> *(He doesn't answer.)*

No? Not gonna tell me? Fine. How about I call Dirk and ask him what happened?

**BOBBY**.  You don't even know him.

**MARIA**.  I think I have a pretty good idea.

**BOBBY**.  He's not a bad guy, Ma. He just.

**MARIA**.  What? He just what? What does he just?

**BOBBY**.  *(Dismissing.)* This is none of your business.

**MARIA**.  You *are* my business. Everything about you is my business!

**BOBBY**.  It wasn't his fault! I. I said some stuff that I shouldn't have. And. Uhh. We had been – drinking. And doing –

> *(He stops midsentence. A loaded glance passes between them.)*

Things. Just. Got out of hand. It was nothing.

**MARIA**.  That doesn't look like nothing.

**BOBBY**.  We had a fight. He apologized. It's over.

MARIA. How many times?

BOBBY. Huh?

MARIA. How many times has he pulled this shit?

BOBBY. *(Looking away.)* Just once.

MARIA. *(Points to her face.)* No-no-no. In the eyes, mister. You tell me in the eyes.

*(He reluctantly does so.)*

How many times?

BOBBY. Once. *(Then with difficulty.)* Twice maybe. I don't know.

MARIA. What's Dirk's last name?

BOBBY. Why?

MARIA. I'm going to call his mother.

BOBBY. And say what??

MARIA. That her son has been bullying my son and I think she needs to have a talk with him.

BOBBY. We're not in second grade, Ma. We're adults!

MARIA. This is how I taught you to be an adult??

BOBBY. I'm not doing this with you.

MARIA. They're all the same. Doesn't matter that they treat you like shit. As long as they look good on your arm.

BOBBY. You're wrong!

MARIA. And you're shallow!

BOBBY. You just hate that I'm happy.

MARIA. *This* is happy?? Tell him to break your arm next time so I can see you ecstatic!

BOBBY. You're just jealous.

**MARIA.** Of what?

**BOBBY.** *That I have someone now and you don't!*

(*Beat.*)

**MARIA.** I'm gonna let that one slide. 'Cause this Dirk clearly has you under some kind of – *influence.*

(*He turns away.*)

Bobby. There is nothing. *Nothing.* I want more than to see you with someone. But this punk ain't it.

**BOBBY.** I love him.

**MARIA.** Ohh, please. That's what you said about the last one. And the guy before that. And the guy before him.

**BOBBY.** So, I haven't had great luck with guys.

**MARIA.** Newsflash, Bobby! *It ain't them!*

(*He lets that sink in, hurt.*)

Okay. So. Here's what we're gonna do. You are going to pick up that phone and whatever self-esteem you have left and you're going to tell that sonofabitch to get lost.

**BOBBY.** Ma.

**MARIA.** Pick up the phone.

**BOBBY.** You can't tell me what to do.

**MARIA.** I can. And I am. Pick up the phone.

**BOBBY.** I'm not breaking up with him.

**MARIA.** You pick up that phone right now or –

**BOBBY.** (*Challenging her.*) Or you'll *what?*

(*Beat.*)

**MARIA.** You pick up that phone. Or you stop calling me.

**BOBBY**. Ohhh. That is just classic you.

**MARIA**.
And no more sending you money. I won't pay your rent. Bills. Credit cards.

**BOBBY**.
I don't need –

You offered to do all that!

You will not see me as long as you are still seeing him.

This is so screwed up.

Pick up the phone.

No!

Pick up the phone!

NO!

PICK UP THE GODDAMN PHONE!

**BOBBY**. NO! FUCK YOU, MA! ALRIGHT? JUST FUCK YOU!

(*Pause. She slowly gets up from the chair, starts to leave, turns back.*)

**MARIA**. (*Becoming emotional.*) I know you may not think you're worth all that much right now. But to me. You are *everything*. I hope someday you can see that you are everything as well.

(*She exits.*)

## Scene Eight

## "If Your Phone Doesn't Ring, It's Me"

**MARIA**.  *(Voice-over.)* Do I speak now?

**BOBBY**.  *(Voice-over. Softly, rushing her.)* Yeah. It's on. Go.

**MARIA**.  *(Voice-over.)* You sure it's on?

**BOBBY**.  *(Voice-over.)* It's on. Go.

**MARIA**.  *(Voice-over.)* Oh. Okay. Umm. You've reached the Collavechio residence. This is Maria. Please leave your name, a message, and about what time you called at the sound of the tone and I will get back to you as soon as I –

**BOBBY**.  *(Voice-over.)* Wrap it up, Ma.

**MARIA**.  *(Voice-over.)* Huh?

**BOBBY**.  *(Voice-over.)* Wrap it up, you're gonna run out of time.

**MARIA**.  *(Voice-over.)* Why are you interrupting me? That's why we have to keep doing this thing over and over and –

*(Beep. Spotlight on **BOBBY**.)*

**BOBBY**.  Hey Ma. It's me. Calling again. Look, I'm sorry I said all those things. But you can't just force me to – we're actually doing a lot better. Dirk got a job. This off-Broadway show. Well. Off-*off* Broadway. Anyway. Call me. If you want.

*(Beep. Another light finds **BOBBY**.)*

Happy Easter, Ma. You're probably already at Church. I've been calling 'cause we wanted to come to Connecticut today. The two of us. We were just gonna show up but then Frankie said not to come because he didn't want a big to-do in front of the kids. So. I guess we'll just stay in the city. Would you just call me already?

*(Beep. And another light.)*

Hey Ma. It's Bobby. I know you're there. It's two o'clock. I know you're watching your stories. Would you just pick up the phone? You know how crazy I get when we don't talk. Alright. We'll just keep doing this then.

*(Beep. Another light.)*

Ma. It's me. You can answer the phone. I'm not seeing Dirk anymore.

*(Lights change as **MARIA** enters.)*

**MARIA.** You finally broke up with him!

**BOBBY.** *(Sadly.)* He actually broke up with me.

*(**BOBBY** plops down on the floor. **MARIA** notices his depressed state.)*

**MARIA.** Tell Mommy what happened.

**BOBBY.** He wanted an open relationship.

**MARIA.** What's that? You don't close the doors in your apartment?

**BOBBY.** An open relationship means that we can each see other people.

**MARIA.** Then he wanted to be single again.

**BOBBY.** No.

**MARIA.** Then he wanted to just be with you.

**BOBBY.** No.

**MARIA.** Then I'm not following.

**BOBBY**.  He wanted to keep seeing me but be able to have sex with other guys.

**MARIA**.  Pigs and animals.

**BOBBY**.  He was screwing around on me the whole time.

**MARIA**.  You know, I really thought I couldn't hate this little shit any more than I already do. Seems like now I can.

**BOBBY**.  That's not exactly Christian behavior.

**MARIA**.  Oh please. You think Jesus liked everyone He hung around with? If Christ had chosen better friends, He wouldn't have died so young.

**BOBBY**.  So. Go on. Let's hear it.

**MARIA**.  Let's hear what?

**BOBBY**.  Tell me you told me so.

**MARIA**.  Sweetheart, I would never say that to you. (But I told you so.)

(*Beat.*)

And the drugs?

**BOBBY**.  How did you find out about that?

**MARIA**.  When I didn't go through your things I might not have found something.

**BOBBY**.  (*Opening up.*) I feel.

**MARIA**.  What baby? What do you feel?

**BOBBY**.  That I'm going to go through my entire life alone. That I'm never going to amount to anything or leave anything behind. That every dream I ever had is going to stay just that. A dream. And no one will ever know who I was or what I wanted to be – or if I even existed.

(*Beat.*)

You got nothing to say to that?

**MARIA.** You don't want to hear what I have to say.

**BOBBY.** I do.

**MARIA.** Trust me. You don't.

**BOBBY.** I want to hear.

**MARIA.** You want to hear?

**BOBBY.** I want to hear.

**MARIA.** Woo-woo-woo.

**BOBBY.** Woo-woo-what?

**MARIA.** Woo-woo-woo.

**BOBBY.** Woo-woo-woo?

**MARIA.** Woo-woo-woo.

**BOBBY.** That's not even a thing.

**MARIA.** Oh, it's a thing.

**BOBBY.** Woo-woo-woo?

**MARIA.** Woo-woo-woo. As in *(Mocking him.)* "Woo-woo-woo, I don't have a boyfriend. Woo-woo-woo, I don't have a job. Woo-woo-woo, my life is going nowhere."

**BOBBY.** Alright, stop. I get it.

**MARIA.** That's just it. You *don't.* Bobby, why did you move to New York?

**BOBBY.** I don't know.

**MARIA.** Sure you do.

**BOBBY.** To become a playwright.

**MARIA.** When was the last time you picked up a pen?

**BOBBY.** It's not that easy.

**MARIA.**  Nothing worthwhile ever is. Look. I don't know from what you do. Me? I had two jobs in life. Be a wife. And be a mother. But you? You've got this agita in you. I don't know what it is or where it comes from. But it's always been there. And I did everything in my power to make it go away. But it never did. And maybe there's a reason for that.

**BOBBY.**  What do you mean?

**MARIA.**  Sweetheart, if you can somehow tap into whatever the hell you have been feeling all these years – what you are feeling *right now* – hone in on *that* – because if you do – that agita may just lead you to your dream.

**BOBBY.**  I don't even know what I would write about.

**MARIA.**  Anything you put on paper will be better than the nothing you have so far.

**BOBBY.**  I guess I can write about my breakup.

**MARIA.**  NO! No one wants to see a play about a bad relationship! That's why I hated *The Carousel*.

**BOBBY.**  It's just *Carousel*, Ma. No "the."

**MARIA.**  Stupid play. He beats up his wife, dies, comes back down from heaven, slaps his daughter and she's all like "Oh it felt like a kiss..." If that little girl doesn't know the difference between a slap and a kiss, she's got bigger problems than having a dead father!

**BOBBY.**  Alright. No bad relationship plays.

**MARIA.**  *(Gasps loudly.)* Why don't you write a nice play about us?!

**BOBBY.**  *(Laughs.)* Us? Ma. No one's gonna come to see a play about you and me.

**MARIA.**  I'm not talking "us" us – as in "you and me us." I'm talking "us" as in – a play about a mother and her son.

**BOBBY.**  That's already been done.

**MARIA.** *Not by you it hasn't.*

**BOBBY.** It's impossible to get a play produced in New York.

**MARIA.** Nothing is impossible in our family! Your grandfather.

**BOBBY.** Please don't tell that story.

**MARIA.** He came to this country with only the shirt on his back.

**BOBBY.** And she's off.

**MARIA.** He took a room in a boarding house. Sold vegetables in a little cart with wheels. Like Tevye. Now that musical I liked.

**BOBBY.** Of course you did. It had a loud mother.

(*Beat.*)

**MARIA.** Pick up the pen.

## Scene Nine

## "That's My Kid Up There"

*(In the darkness we hear audience laughter:
Then:)*

**ACTRESS.** *(Voice-over.)* How did you get to New York?

**ACTOR.** *(Voice-over.)* Oh. Well. Johnny thought –

**ACTRESS.** *(Voice-over.)* Listen to me, mister. I am on the verge of obtaining a severe mental illness right now! I have seven other kids at home and a dog who is incontinent! If you mention Johnny's name one more time, and I do mean ONE MORE TIME – there may not be a dog alive when you get home!

> *(Lights up on **MARIA** and **BOBBY** sitting side by side in theatre seats. He is wearing a tux. She is in a dress.)*

**ACTRESS.** *(Voice-over.)* Now. How did you get from Connecticut to New York?

**ACTOR.** *(Voice-over.)* We took the train.

**ACTRESS.** *(Voice-over.)* Where did you get the money to take the train?

> *(Beaming with pride, **MARIA** looks at **BOBBY**, then straight ahead.)*

**ACTOR.** *(Voice-over.)* Well, Johnny thought –

**ACTRESS.** *(Voice-over.)* Frankie, I mean it! I've got Skippy on a choke collar. I can finish him off by the time I stop speaking this sentence! Now. *(Pointedly.)* Where did you get the money for the train?

**ACTOR.** *(Voice-over. Sadly.)* I sold the gold crucifix you and Daddy got me for my communion.

*(Overwhelmed with gratitude, **BOBBY** looks to **MARIA**, then straight ahead.)*

*(Voice-over.)* I didn't think you'd let me come back home so I sold my crucifix to get train tickets for me and – you know who. That's why I ran away. Because I thought you and Daddy would hate me.

*(Still looking forward, **MARIA** takes **BOBBY**'s hand in hers. We hear the sound of curtain call applause. **MARIA** stands, clapping and whistling. **BOBBY** looks up to her, eventually stands as well.)*

*(The lights change. The play is over.)*

**BOBBY.** So. Go on. Let's hear it.

**MARIA.** *(Affectionately.)* I told you so.

**BOBBY.** Seriously. What did you think?

**MARIA.** I think the actress playing me looked much older than I do.

**BOBBY.** *(Appeasing her.)* Oh, definitely.

**MARIA.** And her voice was a little husky.

**BOBBY.** *(Amused.)* I will give her that note.

**MARIA.** And I could have done without that shirtless scene.

**BOBBY.** *(Fishing.)* Anything else?

*(Beat.)*

**MARIA.** It's good, Bobby. Really good.

*(**BOBBY** is embarrassed by the compliment, smiles. **MARIA** notices.)*

Upp. There it is.

**BOBBY.**  What?

**MARIA.**  You. Smiling. Keep that shit up. It looks good on you.

(**MARIA** *starts off.*)

**BOBBY.**  Where you going?

**MARIA.**  To the ladies' room before I burst! You couldn't have written a nice intermission??

(**MARIA** *starts off, turns back.*)

Did I tell you how proud I am of you?

**BOBBY.**  Not yet.

**MARIA.**  I'll save it for the party.

(*She exits.*)

(*Lights change as the curtain call applause returns, growing louder and louder to deafening, echoing, bizarre levels. A series of blinding flashbulbs go off as we hear the sound tape speed up rapidly and the flashing lights increase in frequency. Then darkness.*)

## Scene Ten

## "You Are Going To Drive Me To Drink"

*(A morose* **BOBBY** *is sitting at a table. After a moment, a chipper* **MARIA** *enters.)*

**MARIA.** I. Am having. The best. Time!

*(**BOBBY** slowly looks to **MARIA**, then away.)*

You want to know what I did this morning? Let me tell you what I did this morning. It started with all us family members sitting in a circle. And then one by one we each had to say why we were here. I was kind of feeling a little sorry for myself. Until I heard all of *their* stories. Oh. My. God. Bobby. You wouldn't *believe* the things I heard today. But we were given very strict instructions not to tell any of this to anyone. So, I can only repeat this once:

*(She takes a seat at the table.)*

First up were the Carmichaels. Nice couple from one of the Dakotas. Not all that interesting. *But their daughter?* She's like this overeater? And she was doing pretty well on her program until she relapsed. Guess what she relapsed on. Forget it. You'll never guess. That girl ate two and a half boxes of dry Duncan Hines cake mix! She's so addicted to food she couldn't even wait forty minutes to bake the cake!

Then there's Lucinda Wilton. A widow like me. Now Lucinda comes from money. Texas money. The only problem is that her son is this raging alcoholic who likes to go to the casinos when he is drunk and spend all of Lucinda's money on roulette. Her son has been to Betty Ford *thirteen times*. I did the math in my head.

**MARIA.**  She's spent at least half a million dollars trying to get that kid of hers sober. I mean, for that kind of money she should just buy a new kid!

But my favorites, oh my favorites are the Rosenbergs. Mort and Edie. Good people. Like us. But Jews. Real Jews. The Hasidic kind. Their son is like a rabbi. Has this lovely wife. Three beautiful girls. Nice home. Everything you can wish for in a son. But at night? When he tells his wife he's going out to study the Torah? He's really smoking crack and kissing Black transexuals. I mean, imagine being his mother and trying to explain THAT to the ladies of Temple Beth Shalom!

Oh, and then there's –

**BOBBY.**  *(Snapping.)* I DON'T CARE! WOULD YOU JUST SHUT UP?!

*(Awkward silence. Then:)*

What did you tell them about me?

**MARIA.**  Not much.

**BOBBY.**  You must have said something.

**MARIA.**  I kept it vague. All I said was that you had this – cute little psychotic break.

**BOBBY.**  I just want to die.

**MARIA.**  Well, you're not going to. So stop being so dramatic.

**BOBBY.**  I hate it here.

**MARIA.**  Are you kidding? I would love to *move* here. Great weather. Three meals a day. Two snacks.

**BOBBY.**  Can I come home?

**MARIA.**  N! O!

**BOBBY.**  Suppose people find out.

**MARIA.** What's to find out? That a gay man working in the theatre is getting help for a drug problem?? *Shocker! (Then, softer.)* I don't understand how this happened. Dammit Bobby. You were doing so good. What made you pick up that shit again?

**BOBBY.** Drop it.

**MARIA.** Tell me.

**BOBBY.** You're gonna yell.

**MARIA.** I won't yell.

**BOBBY.** I got back together with Dirk.

**MARIA.** *(Making a face then calmly.)* Okay. Good. Great. You got back together with Dirk. See? I'm not yelling. I mean, why would I possibly *(Immediately insane.)* FUCKING YELL AT YOU?!!

**BOBBY.** Would you keep your voice down?

**MARIA.** You think I care what people think of me in this clown car?!

**BOBBY.** I knew I shouldn't have told you.

**MARIA.** What were you thinking?!

**BOBBY.** It wasn't my fault!

**MARIA.** Ohhhh. You are so lucky we're in a rehab right now or I would be drinking wine from the box!

**BOBBY.** I didn't expect it to happen.

**MARIA.** I didn't expect to get pregnant with you. *Look where our choices got us.*

**BOBBY.** It's not like I planned it. I just ran into him. He was walking toward me down the same sidewalk. What was I supposed to do?

**MARIA.** Oh, I don't know. *Cross the street maybe?!*

**BOBBY**.  He was all dressed up. Looking so good. We talked. I walked him home. One thing led to another. And.

**MARIA**.  And you two have sex and I'm the one getting fucked! Stuck with a fifty-thousand-dollar rehab bill!

**BOBBY**.  We only got back together for a few weeks. And then.

**MARIA**.  No. Wait. Let me guess. He cheated.

**BOBBY**.  He had a boyfriend the whole time.

**MARIA**.  Ta-da.

**BOBBY**.  So. He went back to him –

**MARIA**.  – and you went back to the crystal light.

**BOBBY**.  Crystal meth.

(*Beat.*)

I'm just so tired, Ma. I don't want to be hurt. I don't want to be happy. I don't want to be sad. I don't want to be sorry. I don't want to think. I don't want to know. *I just want to be numb.*

**MARIA**.  Well, you can't be! That's not how life works. We don't get to check out whenever we want so knock it off.

**BOBBY**.  I don't know what you're getting so worked up about? I'm the one who's stuck here. Not you.

**MARIA**.  I'm not here? *I'm not here.*

(*She gets up from the table, her intensity building.*)

I'm not the one who got the call at four in the morning telling me my son was batshit crazy and filled up with more amphetamines than a CVS. *I'm not here?*

I'm not the one who bailed your ass out of jail and paid that hotshot lawyer ten grand to get your misdemeanor down to a violation. *I'm not here?*

I'm not the one who abandoned the rest of my family so I can fly three thousand miles just to have my son turn around and tell me *I'm not here*! Let me tell *you* something, mister: I've *always* been here. And you know what I'm beginning to think? *You don't deserve me to be.*

    *(Pause. Then:)*

**BOBBY**. *(In a boy-like cry.)* That was meeeeeaaan.

    *(**MARIA** throws up her hands to God.)*

**MARIA**. I don't know what to do with you, Bobby. I really don't know what else to do. I gave you everything. More than all the other kids combined. I gave you things in me I didn't even know I had. And for what? So, you can bitch about your shitty life? No one has a better life than you!

You wanted to move to New York? You moved to New York. You wanted to be a playwright? You became a playwright. You wanted to be on Broadway? You were on Broadway. But you don't want good things to happen to you because you're so hellbent on screwing them up! You're so damn busy looking for the thing.

**BOBBY**. What thing?

**MARIA**. The thing. The thing. Either *this* is gonna be the thing. Or *that* is gonna be the thing. Or *over there* is gonna be the thing. *(Then reflectively.)* The thing about the thing? The thing is never the thing.

And until you get that, until you finally figure out who the hell you are and that your worth cannot be negotiated by some guy or some play or some outside whatever – until you get all that and really believe it – you're just gonna have a lifetime of the woo-woo-woos.

**BOBBY**. So then what now?

**MARIA**. I can't answer that for you. But maybe? If you try to figure out who you don't want to be? You might just fall into who you are.

**BOBBY**. That's pretty deep for a woman who still has shag carpeting.

**MARIA**. Shut up. It's the only rug you can rake.

> *(They both share a smile. A bell rings.)*

I've got to get to my next workshop.

> *(She pulls out a folded piece of paper from her pocketbook.)*

*(Reading.)* "Denial Is Not A River In Egypt."

> *(She doesn't understand that. Then does.)*

*(Laughs.)* Oh. That's funny.

> *(She walks away, turns back.)*

You used to love the merry-go-round. Remember? As a kid you were so happy and looked so cute going around and around in circles. But as an adult? You just look pathetic. Get off the ride, Bobby.

> *(She exits.)*

## Scene Eleven

## "Who Wants To Go Bye-Bye?"

*(A long white hospital curtain is drawn.* **BOBBY** *is standing outside.)*

**BOBBY.** How you coming, Ma?

**MARIA.** *(Calling from behind the curtain.)* I'm putting on my face.

**BOBBY.** I've seen you without your face before.

**MARIA.** The grandkids are stopping by. I don't want to scare them. So I'm putting on my face. You didn't have play practice today?

**BOBBY.** We don't call it play practice, Ma.

**MARIA.** What do you call it?

**BOBBY.** Rehearsal.

**MARIA.** Do you practice the play at rehearsal?

**BOBBY.** Yeah.

**MARIA.** Then it's play practice.

**BOBBY.** I don't have to be there today.

**MARIA.** Why? Did you get fired?

**BOBBY.** No, Ma. I didn't get fired.

**MARIA.** Did you steal? You got fired for stealing?

**BOBBY.** I didn't steal, Ma.

**MARIA.** You stole something at play practice?

**BOBBY.** There's nothing to steal at play practice.

**MARIA.** I thought you called it "rehearsals"?

**BOBBY.**  They are rehearsals.

**MARIA.**  Then why did you call it play practice?

**BOBBY.**  Because you called it play practice.

**MARIA.**  I think I like rehearsals better.

(*Beat.*)

**BOBBY.**  You okay in there?

**MARIA.**  Yeah. You can come in now.

(**BOBBY** *pulls back the curtain to reveal* **MARIA.** *She is bald, frail, and sick.*)

There's my boy.

(*He kisses her.*)

(*Self-conscious.*) How do I look?

**BOBBY.**  Beautiful.

**MARIA.**  (*Pointing.*) In the eyes. Tell me in the eyes.

**BOBBY.**  (*Looking in her eyes.*) You. Are. Gorgeous.

**MARIA.**  (*Sweetly.*) Liar.

**BOBBY.**  How you feeling?

**MARIA.**  I'm not going to dance the Tarantella, that's for sure. These treatments knock the shit out of me.

**BOBBY.**  You're doing great.

**MARIA.**  I'm doing great. I got everyone saying I'm doing great. Why don't I feel great?

**BOBBY.**  You're gonna beat this thing.

**MARIA.**  That critic from *The New York Times* was right. You really *haven't* met a cliche you didn't like.

**BOBBY.**  I got my closing notice at the opening night party with that show.

**MARIA.** No offense. But even that was too late.

(*They share a smile.*)

Want to hear something funny?

**BOBBY.** Sure.

**MARIA.** Last night. I was saying my prayers. And halfway through the "Our Father" – I just – I couldn't remember the rest of it. Just forgot. Funny, huh? With all the Masses I attended. And the Communions. And the rosaries I said for you kids over all these years – you think I would know it by now.

**BOBBY.** You still pray every day?

**MARIA.** It takes me forty-nine minutes to get through all my prayers. Thirty-eight if one of you kids pisses me off.

(*She taps the seat beside her.*)

Sit down. I need to tell you something.

(*He sits down on the bed beside her.*)

And I don't want you to get mad.

**BOBBY.** I won't get mad.

**MARIA.** Promise?

**BOBBY.** Swear to God. What is it?

(*Beat and then:*)

**MARIA.** I did kill Tippy. I mean, not directly. He was just making me so crazy. Running all over the house. Making a mess out of everything. Do you know how hard it is to get shit out of a shag carpet?

**BOBBY.** I would assume it's time consuming.

**MARIA.**  I just couldn't take it anymore. So. I brought him to the Humane Society in the hope that maybe another family would adopt him. But after a month – after I saw how heartbroken you still were – I drove up there to get Tippy back. But it was too late. They already put him down because no one else wanted him.

**BOBBY.**  That's alright, Ma. Tippy and I had some good times together.

**MARIA.**  You're not mad?

**BOBBY.**  I'm not mad.

**MARIA.**  Good. 'Cause there's more.

        (**BOBBY** *settles himself.*)

Remember Herbie? That gerbil Mrs. Kowalski gave you to take care of over Christmas vacation?

**BOBBY.**  The one you suddenly decided to give to your cousin Jenny who had cerebral palsy and wanted a low maintenance pet?

**MARIA.**  I don't have a cousin Jenny.

**BOBBY.**  *(Fidgeting.)* Go on.

**MARIA.**  When you were sledding with your friends? Herbie chewed his way out of the cardboard box and got loose in the house. And I just got so scared.

**BOBBY.**  So, what did you do?

**MARIA.**  I picked him up by the tail and flushed him down the toilet.

**BOBBY.**  Awwww, Jesus! Ma!

**MARIA.**  Gerbils are diseased. They carry the Black Plague.

**BOBBY.**  The Black Plague was centuries ago.

**MARIA.**  History always repeats itself.

**BOBBY.**  Amazing.

**MARIA**. You mad?

**BOBBY**. Not really.

**MARIA**. Good. 'Cause there's more.

**BOBBY**. HOW CAN THERE BE –? *(He stops himself, then calmly.)* Go on.

**MARIA**. Remember that boy you liked so much at school. The one that looked like one of the von Trapp kids? That's another musical I didn't like. Nuns should stay nuns.

**BOBBY**. What boy are you talking about?

**MARIA**. The one who lived on Montowese Street.

**BOBBY**. Peter Donovan?

**MARIA**. Yeah.

**BOBBY**. What? Did you kill him too?

**MARIA**. Remember his mother?

**BOBBY**. Yeah. She passed away when I was in high school.

**MARIA**. She had the same thing I have.

**BOBBY**. Yeah. But Ma, that was a while ago and –

**MARIA**. Let me finish. And don't get mad.

**BOBBY**. I won't get mad.

**MARIA**. Promise.

**BOBBY**. I already swore to God. But technically that was just for Tippy which turned into Herbie and a handicapped cousin that doesn't exist so I don't know where we are with this anymore.

**MARIA**. Bobby. I'm.

*(She stops midsentence.)*

**MARIA.** I'm not going to have any more of these treatments. After I finish this one? I'm done.

**BOBBY.** What? Why?

**MARIA.** I just want to go home. Spend time with you. Your brothers. Sisters. The grandkids. Maybe not so much the grandkids. I just don't want to spend my remaining time here in these hospitals.

**BOBBY.** Ma, if you don't finish these treatments –

**MARIA.** Sweetheart. I'm a seventy-six-year-old woman. And seventy-six ain't bad.

**BOBBY.** Seventy-seven would be better.

**MARIA.** Then let's shoot for that. What the hell. Let's shoot for eighty. But if eighty doesn't happen. If seventy-seven doesn't happen. I need you to be okay with that. Alright?

    *(He nods. Beat.)*

I want a closed casket.

**BOBBY.** No. I need to see you during all this.

**MARIA.** I don't want people to see me without my hair.

**BOBBY.** Then we'll do a wig. I can get Tom to create one. He designed the wigs for my last show.

**MARIA.** I liked those wigs. Have him make my hair nice and high like in the sixties.

**BOBBY.** I'll tell him.

**MARIA.** And make sure Paulie Junior does my make-up and not Paulie Senior. Paulie Senior had your Aunt Concetta looking like a street walker.

**BOBBY.** No Paulie Senior.

**MARIA.** I also bought a new dress. It's hanging in my closet. That's the dress I want to be buried in.

**BOBBY**.  How am I going to know which one it is?

**MARIA**.  I safety-pinned a sign on it that says "This Is The Dress I Want To Be Buried In." I already picked out my casket.

**BOBBY**.  When did you do that?

**MARIA**.  I was feeling pretty good last month so I had Johnny drive me over to Genovese. I tried them all out.

**BOBBY**.  *You got into them??*

**MARIA**.  How am I supposed to know if they're comfortable?

(**BOBBY** *shakes his head in disbelief.*)

Pick out some nice music for the service. The "Ave Maria." The "Be Not Afraid." Oh. And I want you to let little Gina play her flute at the funeral.

**BOBBY**.  Ma, when little Gina plays that thing, it sounds like the mating call of a beluga whale.

(**MARIA** *shoots him a look.*)

Fine. Little Gina will play the flute. What else?

**MARIA**.  I want you to say my eulogy.

(*She then retrieves a folded piece of paper from her nightgown pocket. Hands it to him.*)

**BOBBY**.  Amazing.

**MARIA**.  I was a good mother to you.

**BOBBY**.  Naah. You were the best.

**MARIA**.  See, it's sayings like that that make the critics not like you.

(*He smiles at her, then suddenly begins crying.*)

**MARIA**.  Awwww, sweetheart. No-no-no. Come here.

> *(He puts his head in her lap as he weeps uncontrollably.)*

Shh-Shh-Shh. *(Trying to hold it together.)* I'm gonna try to hold on as long as I can. But at some point. I'm going to have to let go. And you're going to have to *let* me let go. Okay?

> *(He nods.)*

You're going to get through this. We're both going to get through this.

# Epilogue

*(In the darkness we hear an extremely bad flute rendition of "Ave Maria.")*

*(Music fades as the lights come up on a cemetery.* **BOBBY,** *now more than a decade older, is grooming the plot.)*

*(After a moment,* **MARIA** *appears behind him. She is wearing a white pantsuit. She looks radiant.)*

**MARIA.**  It's about time you cleaned things up. Those weeds were getting so tall I was starting to give them confirmation names.

**BOBBY.**  What are you doing down here again?

**MARIA.**  My hair appointment got cancelled.

**BOBBY.**  They have hair salons in heaven?

**MARIA.**  Just the one. It's called – "The Hairafter."

*(She edges closer.)*

You look good.

**BOBBY.**  Ehh. I got old. Although age is just a number.

**MARIA.**  See? It's that. The critics don't like that.

**BOBBY.**  So, you keep telling me.

**MARIA.**  I saw your friend Dirk the other day.

**BOBBY.**  Yeah. I heard he had passed away.

---

*A license to produce *Conversations with Mother* does not include a performance license for any third-party or copyrighted recordings. Licensees should create their own.

**MARIA.**  I was playing cards with him last week and guess what?

**BOBBY & MARIA.**  He cheated.

**MARIA.**  How's Trent?

**BOBBY.**  He's good. I'm trying to get him to retire but his practice keeps expanding.

**MARIA.**  You finally marry a doctor and I'm not around to brag about it.

**BOBBY.**  You would have liked him, Ma.

**MARIA.**  Italian?

**BOBBY.**  Polish.

**MARIA.**  Catholic?

**BOBBY.**  Agnostic.

**MARIA.**  We can stop right there.

(*Beat.*)

How are the twins?

**BOBBY.**  Just started college.

**MARIA.**  They behaving?

**BOBBY.**  Elizabeth? Yes. But Christopher? I don't know what the hell I'm going to do with that kid. He just can't seem to stay out of trouble. Always has a story. Never his fault. Keeps expecting me to send him money.

**MARIA.**  No DNA test needed there.

**BOBBY.**  Come on. I wasn't that bad.

(*Beat.*)

**MARIA.**  (*Cryptically.*) Are you happy, sweetheart?

**BOBBY.**  I have a man who adores me. A nice family. A beautiful home –

**MARIA.** I didn't ask what you had. Bobby. Are you happy?

**BOBBY.** Yeah. I think I just might be.

*(The sound of thunder can be heard.)*

**MARIA.** That's my cue.

**BOBBY.** Nooo. Just a little longer, Ma.

**MARIA.** Come on. Let me walk you to your car.

*(The thunder gets louder.)*

*(To God.)* I SAID. I AM WALKING. MY SON. TO HIS CAR!

*(The thunder gets softer.)*

*(With difficulty.)* Listen. Sweetheart. As we walk to the car. I'm going to need you to hold my hand. Alright?

**BOBBY.** Yeah. Sure, Ma.

**MARIA.** *(Gently.)* Because you're not going to make it all the way to the car.

*(He turns to look at her.)*

I'm sorry, sweetheart.

**BOBBY.** No.

**MARIA.** Come on.

**BOBBY.** No. I'm not going.

**MARIA.** You're going.

**BOBBY.** You can't make me.

**MARIA.** I was sent by God. I actually think I can.

*(Loud thunder.)*

*(To God.)* WE ARE COMING! SETTLE DOWN!!

*(Beat.)*

**BOBBY.** I've just been – overtired.

**MARIA.** And the chest pains?

**BOBBY.** From stress.

**MARIA.** The shortness of breath?

**BOBBY.** I have asthma.

**MARIA.** And a doctor husband who told you exactly what this is.

*(Beat.)*

**BOBBY.** Trent.

**MARIA.** Will be fine.

**BOBBY.** My kids.

**MARIA.** Will also be fine.

*(Beat.)*

**BOBBY.** How can I never speak to them again?

(**MARIA** *gives him a look. He suddenly understands.)*

Then. This is it?

*(Beat.)*

**MARIA.** This is it.

**BOBBY.** I'm going to die.

**MARIA.** You're going to die.

**BOBBY.** Today.

**MARIA.** Like in minutes.

**BOBBY.** Not very dramatic.

**MARIA**. What? You'd rather die tragically? Like that Nancy character in *Oliver*? Another show I hated. I mean, clubbing a prostitute to death in a children's musical??

**BOBBY**. Why did you even *go* to the theatre?

**MARIA**. *(Sweetly.)* 'Cause I got to sit next to you.

*(The music begins.)*

Come on. Come dance with your mother.

*(**MARIA** extends herself to **BOBBY**. He grasps her one hand, putting his other around her waist.)*

*(They begin to slow dance to the music. They are smiling and laughing as the music builds. It is euphoric. A son is dancing with his mother.)*

*(Suddenly, **MARIA** pulls away from the dance and begins walking upstage, slowly being pulled by a beautiful, alluring, increasingly bright light. She turns back to **BOBBY**, extending her hand.)*

*(**BOBBY** takes one last glance out into the audience. His look is pained at first, which then turns into joyful acceptance.)*

*(He walks toward **MARIA**, takes her hand, as they both turn and walk toward the now blinding light.)*

*(Blackout.)*

**End of Play**